Karl's Diary

Karl's Diary

It's a Dog's Life

SHARON WINTERS

For information about this title or to order other books and/or electronic media, contact the publisher:

Sharon Winters
http://SharonWinters.com
email: KarlsDiaryBook@Yahoo.com

ISBNs:
979-8-9861004-0-1 (softcover)
979-8-9861004-1-8 (eBook)

Printed in the United States of America

Cover and Interior design: 1106 Design

Dedicated to all of the people who are committed to rescuing animals and finding them forever loving homes. In particular:

The Humane Society of Yuma
  in Yuma, Arizona

Friends for Life Animal Rescue
  in Gilbert, Arizona

Maricopa County Animal Care and Control
  in Mesa and Phoenix, Arizona

Until one has loved an animal,
a part of one's soul remains unawakened.

—ANATOLE FRANCE

Foreword

Serendipity *is often described* as a "happy accident." But its full definition is "the phenomenon of finding valuable or agreeable things not sought for." I make this distinction because both this foreword, and the rest of the book you're about to read, began as serendipitous events.

I met Sharon Winters by way of an email response to an article I wrote for the *Mensa Bulletin* back in 2008. Titled "A Tail of Discovery," it recounted the rescue of a pet rat named Molly, who my husband and I had spotted under a drive-up mailbox in the course of running errands on a snowy first day of spring. How long had she been there? Had others noticed her before us and merely driven past? I don't know. Nor do I know what "accident" had landed her there. I only know that at the moment we arrived, this tiny brown and white creature sat before us, in need of a little help. And when my husband held out a hand, and the grateful gal immediately hopped aboard, I could tell it was the start of a most wondrous "happy" event.

The same might be said of receiving Sharon's email. In it she explained that she, too, was a great lover of animals, and she shared a couple of short tales she had written from the perspective of pet guinea pigs. We bonded instantly. And so began a friendship that has been growing ever since.

Given our commonalities, it came as no surprise when, in early 2015, I received a message from Sharon's email account, written by a new resident of her household—a chocolate-colored dog with golden eyes, who had come to her through his own series of serendipitous events. In the message, he introduced himself as Come Ear Karl. As you will learn on the pages that follow, things were a bit confusing in those first days after his arrival—including his new name. Well, some things were confusing. Others were crystal clear. He now had a family. The food was great. He was dearly loved—and he was home.

I started this foreword by talking about serendipity because the circumstances that brought Molly to me, those that brought Karl to Sharon, those that brought about my friendship with Sharon, and the myriad of others relating to these happy occurrences that space prevents recounting here, were by no means planned—at least—not by me or Sharon. And while all have ultimately proved valuable beyond any description that can be put into words, I don't believe for a minute that any of them were accidents.

Neither do I believe was your picking up this book. I hope you enjoy meeting Karl through this book as much as I enjoyed knowing him as his "auntie." And I hope your own serendipitous journeys lead to all things being as right with your own world as you will see how Karl meeting Sharon made everything right with his world.

—Mil Scott, editor and publisher of: *The Rodent Reader Quarterly*

In December of 2014 I was wandering in the Yuma Desert in Arizona. I was lost, thirsty, and hungry. A kind man saw me and scooped me up into his arms. He took me to The Humane Society of Yuma where I was put up for adoption. People would look at me, but they didn't want me.

After a few weeks I was put into a car and transported to Friends for Life Animal Rescue in Gilbert, Arizona, where I was put into a large kennel with grass and a dog house. People would look at me, but again, no one wanted me. I was feeling unloved and unwanted.

It was New Year's Day, and I still didn't have a family to love me forever; a family I could love forever. I was sitting all alone in my kennel and thinking about what I wished for in the New Year. Should I lose weight? Nah. Read more? Maybe. Work more—NO! Play more? Sure.

Wouldn't it be wonderful if everyone knew they were loved and precious; that the peace that passes all understanding is in the hearts and minds of everyone. With so much love there would be no fear. With so much peace there would be no war. As I was thinking about all of this, a doggy angel appeared before me and asked me if I had a wish. I sat up and gave her my biggest smile. "Yes! I want to go to a home filled with love and peace."

As she fluttered her wings she said, "Make your wish and click your paws three times as you say, 'I want to go home. I want to go home. I want to go home.'"

FEBRUARY 20, 2015

Things soon began to happen. First, a photographer took a beautiful picture of me. Then on February 20, 2015, my picture was published in *The Arizona Republic* with the hope that someone would want me. And that's when it happened! A man and a woman showed up at Friends for Life. I was taken out of my kennel and walked over to a bench. There was a woman sitting on the bench and a man was standing beside her. The man petted me with a loving gentleness. The woman extended her hand to me, and I moved over to her and looked into her eyes. She said, "Do you want to come home with us?" All was right with the world.

MAY 20, 2015

At Friends for Life, someone had named me Porter, but when Mommy and Daddy brought me home, they gave me a new name; a name that would fit a Boykin Spaniel. But what was it? They kept saying, "Wanna Go Potty?" and "Come Ear Karl." Finally, I recognized my new name. It was just Karl. I liked it.

I liked riding in the car, too, and on one of my first long car rides, Daddy drove us to Flagstaff, Arizona. It took three hours and by the time we arrived, I really had to take a walk!

On my first walk in Flagstaff, I found myself in a large forest with a lot of sweet-smelling pine trees and other interesting smells as well as squirrels and singing birds. There was a lot to investigate.

SEPTEMBER 20, 2015

I learned how to get whatever I wanted from my new family. I just give them a certain look. You can see the look I'm talking about in the picture. I would think about what I wanted and POW! I would give them the LOOK. Works for me every time.

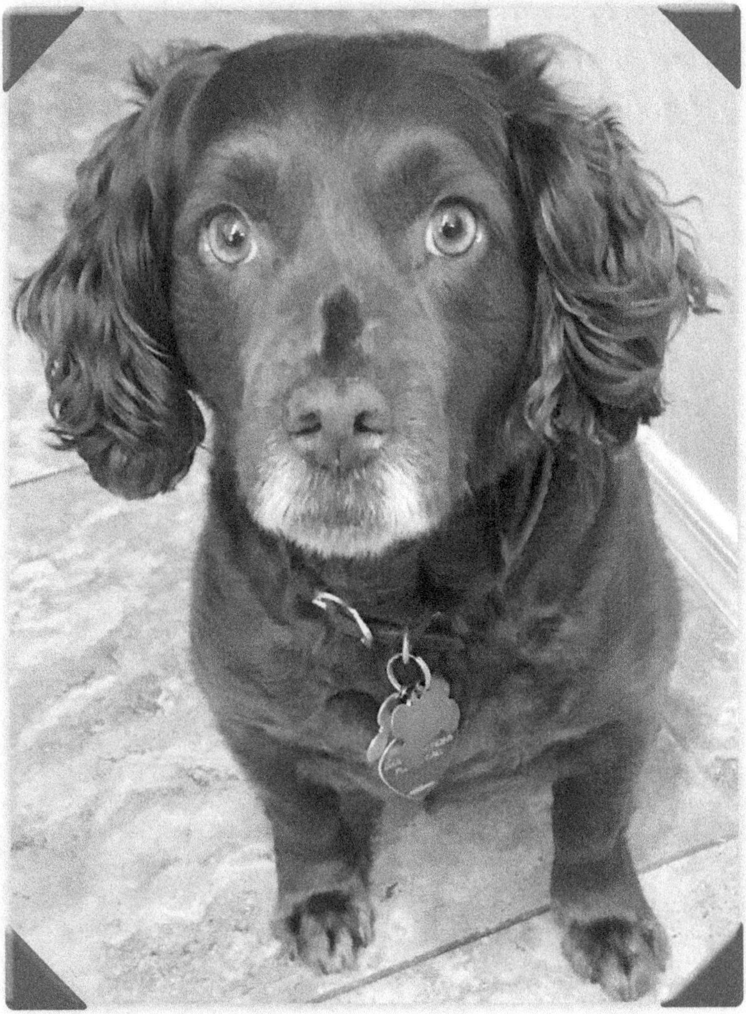

The LOOK.

SEPTEMBER 22, 2015

All Mommy is saying today is, "Who did this?" I turn my back for one minute and the trash can with yummy smells MYSTERIOUSLY turns over. Now I'm in trouble until someone confesses to this deed. Mommy and Daddy know how well I have been trained. Why are they suspicious of me? If someone confesses to this deed, I can have fresh carrot juice with my supper. Thank you in advance.

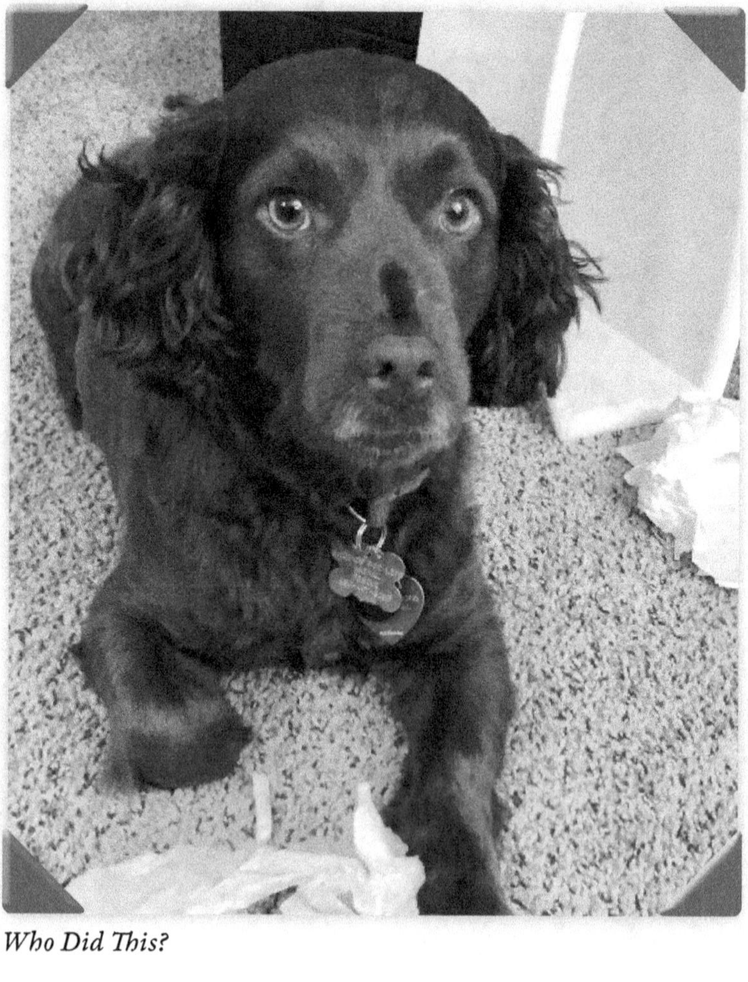

Who Did This?

SEPTEMBER 23, 2015

Someone asked me for advice on how to have a happy life. Here it is: Eat a bug every morning and nothing worse will happen for the rest of the day.

SEPTEMBER 24, 2015

I'm living in the Coconino Forest in Flagstaff, and Daddy takes me for a walk four times a day. I usually see nice people and their dogs on my walks; however, yesterday I met a snotty poodle. I'll call him Mark. As I approached Mark in a friendly manner, Mark gave me a slobbery growl and barked at me. I didn't growl or bark back. I stared at him with my golden eyes and formulated a plan to put him in his place. He continued to snarl at me as his mother pulled him away.

In order to get to the forested area, Daddy and I have to walk down a sidewalk that goes right by Mark's front window where Mark has sentry duty. When I walked up to Mark's window, there he was. He was looking out his window and growling and barking. As I stopped in front of his window, I stared at him with my golden eyes. There was doggy spit flying all over the window as Mark bounced up and down and pawed the glass. I laughed silently as I gave him a steady stare and lifted my leg. I'd taken a big drink of water before we left; so I had plenty to gift to him. Just as I had nothing left to give, his mother came to the window and scolded him for slobbering all over the glass. As hard as his mom tried, she couldn't drag him away from the window; so I knew he was still watching me as I sashayed down the sidewalk and wagged my tail and hips to the rhythm of NAH nah, nah . . . nah NAH . . . nah . . . I get to go to the forest . . . NAH nah, nah . . . nah NAH . . . nah. . . .

Walking in the Coconino Forest.

OCTOBER 22, 2015

    I think I know what life is about now. It's about being snuggled in Daddy's arms and being loved and cared for. And it's about living in a peaceful home—until that cat comes into the backyard and I have to chase her away.

I want to tell you a little secret. When you find someone who loves you unconditionally, make sure they know you love them with all your heart. Here's how you do that: First, look into their eyes and make sure you have their attention. Then move in real close . . . and lick their face.

OCTOBER 27, 2015

Oh my! Mommy discovered I like my ears rubbed while she rocks me in her chair. I'm in a state of rhapsody.

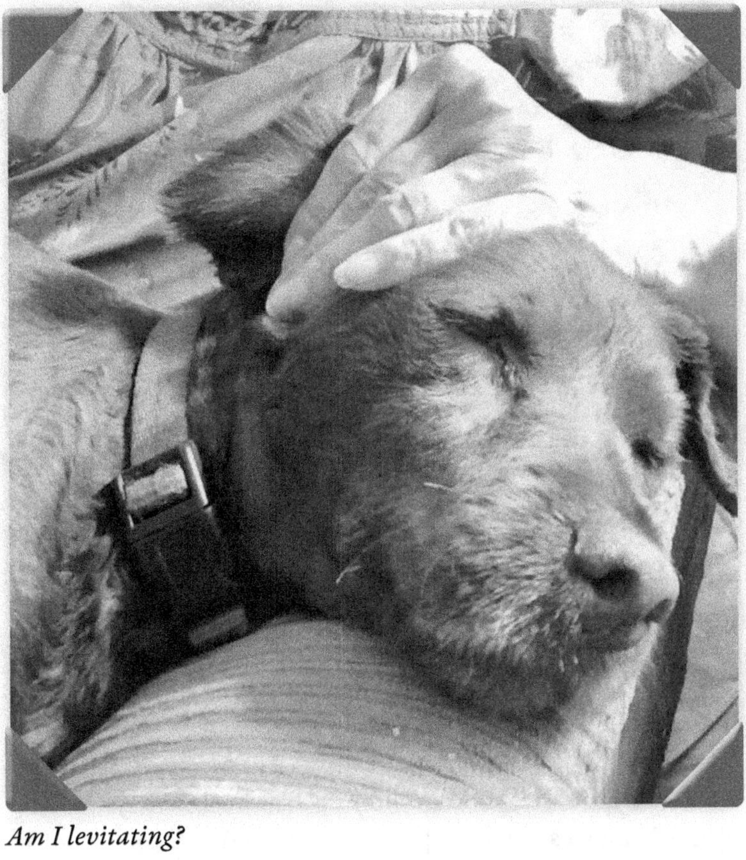

Am I levitating?

DECEMBER 13, 2015

This morning Mommy held me in her arms and rocked me. There is only one purpose in life—to love.

In my special place of feeling loved.

DECEMBER 14, 2015

Daddy was walking me on the sidewalk by a café in downtown Flagstaff, and a school bus pulled up across the street. About six or seven teenage girls stepped out of the bus wearing plaid skirts and white blouses. When the bus pulled away, they all came screaming across the street. Daddy thought they were coming over to see him. NOT! They were looking at me and yelling, "Can we pet him? Can we pet him? He's so cute!" I enjoyed all of the petting and attention.

A teenage boy was watching all of this and came over to my daddy and said, "Sir, what kind of dog is that? He's a babe magnet, and I want one just like him."

DECEMBER 26, 2015

Whew! I got doggy toys for Christmas, and now I'm exhausted from playing with my new toys. I can hardly prop my head up with my paw. I feel like a limp rag.

I'm a spoiled doggy.

I have a little problem. I used to weigh twenty-five pounds and now my Daddy says I weigh twenty-seven pounds. First of all, if this is true, it's not my fault. You see, Mommy and Daddy went out of town for a few days and Uncle Marty took me to his house. I LOVE being at Uncle Marty's house. For one thing, he lets me sleep in his bed, and all night long I snuggle so close to him that I can hear his heart beating. I love that sound and then . . . breakfast!

The first time Uncle Marty put my breakfast kibble in front of me, I gave him a pitiful look, and he said, "What's the matter, Karl? Don't you want to eat your breakfast?" I let my head go limp over my breakfast and then I gave Uncle Marty "The LOOK" with my piercing golden eyes. (I should go into acting.) Uncle Marty scrambled an egg for me and put that over my kibble. Wowzah! That scrambled egg was delicious. I'm drooling just thinking about it. And for dinner we had brisket.

The other thing I like about staying with Uncle Marty is that he works from home, and he has a La-Z-Boy chair for me in his office. I curl up in that chair while he works. In between his phone calls he talks to me about guy stuff, like our walking schedule and what we're having for dinner. Then Uncle Marty takes a break and plays with me. I have a big box of toys at Uncle Marty's house.

So, back to my problem. I heard Mommy telling Daddy that she had a come-to-Jesus talk with Uncle Marty and told him that I'm getting fat. *Excuse me!* Here's the thing. It's winter now and my hair is two inches long in some places, and I know this has added some serious weight. So, in my defense, I'm just saying: I'm NOT fat. I'm fluffy.

I have a smile on my face today because I'm imagining what the world would be like if everybody loved everybody. There would be peace on earth, and bathroom scales would be outlawed.

Outlaw bathroom scales!

JANUARY 10, 2016

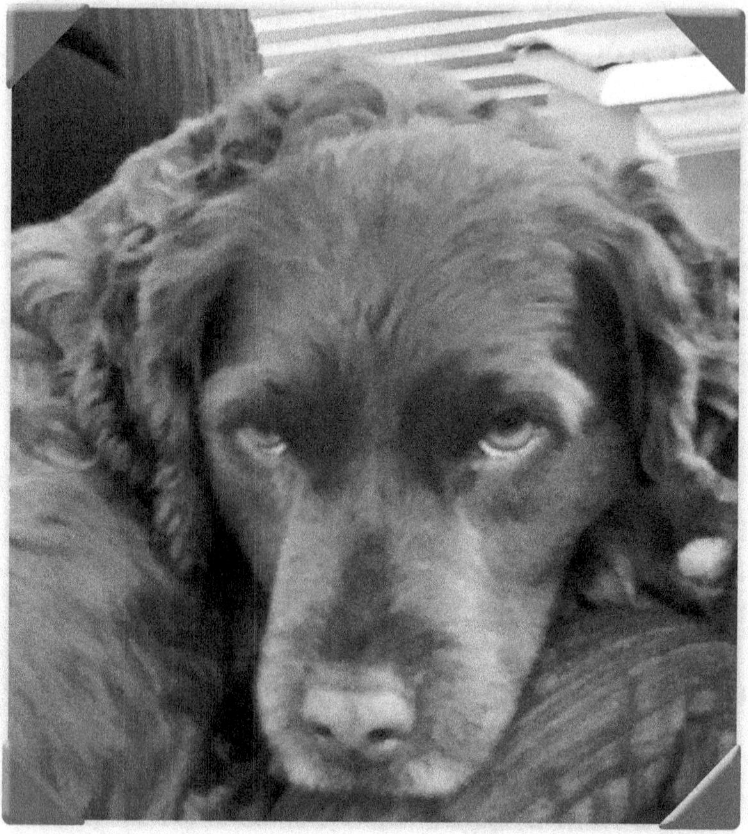

This is my babe magnet look.

JANUARY 16, 2016

Oh! Was I dreaming about steak and lettuce or do I actually smell steak and lettuce? I think I hear Mommy cutting up lettuce leaves and steak. I should check this out . . . Yes! I'm having steak and lettuce for dinner!

JANUARY 23, 2016

I'm not sleeping on the job.

I'm meditating.

My Mommy and Daddy are good friends with our next-door neighbors, Uncle Rick and Auntie Kim. Their dog, Chloe, is my girlfriend. My Daddy and Uncle Rick often take Chloe and me for a walk to the park. I am so in love with Chloe.

I need a haircut. Daddy called me a rag mop this morning, and in front of Chloe, too.

Chloe and I had a wonderful walk to the park this morning. But she won't let me kiss her. Chloe's mother told me that Chloe is playing hard to get. Chloe won't even let me walk her up to

Chloe when she wakes up in the morning.

her front door like any gentle-dog would do. She growls at me. Sigh . . . What's a fella to do?

FEBRUARY 10, 2016

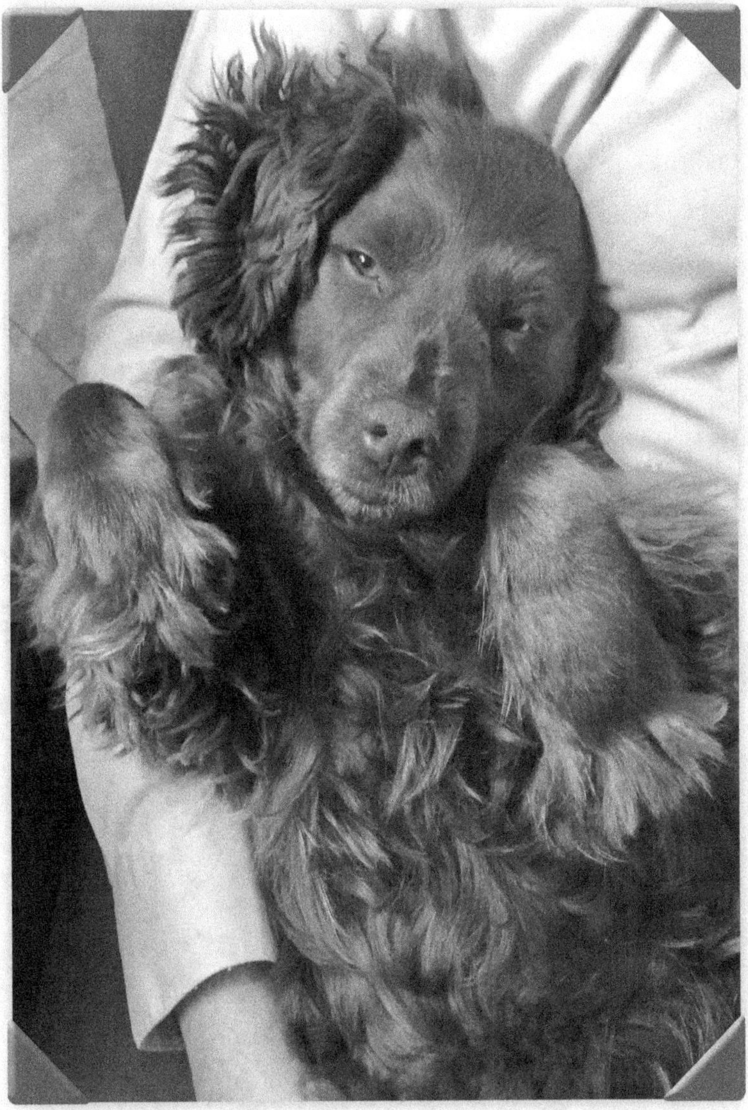

When I'm in Daddy's arms, I'm in heaven.

I heard the doorbell ring, and Chloe was there! She went to the beauty parlor this afternoon and came over to show me how pretty she looks. Wow! She looks stunning. She jumped up on the couch, and I was going to sit with her but then she said she had to go home and eat supper. She didn't let me get close enough to even try to kiss her. I offered her one of my favorite toys, too. It's always something with her . . . sigh . . . I'm so in love.

Chloe looks stunning.

Hey . . . I'm trying to sleep. What's with all the noise? Snoring? Who's snoring? No, no, no . . . I wasn't snoring.

![A dog resting on a cushioned chair looking at the camera]

What woke me up?

Mommy, why is daddy putting a lot of things in the car? You aren't going to forget me, are you? Mommy put my seat belt harness on; so I know I'm going with Mommy and Daddy. I don't know where we are going, but I don't care as long as I'm with my family. I think I'll take a nap and dream of Chloe.

Traveling to Flagstaff.

I was watching this magician on TV, and he did a disappearing magic trick. I thought, I can do that, too.

Now you see me,

now you don't.

No, Mommy! Chloe isn't going back to Chicago, is she? Daddy, I have girl troubles!

Goodbye, Chloe. I love you. I hope you will come back next year.

Come back to me, Chloe!

Chloe Here: I finally managed to escape my dog carrier, and I ran up and down the aisle of the airplane yelling, "Karl! Karl! Karl! We can't take off without Karl!" Nobody understood what I was saying! People up and down the aisle were trying to grab me. Finally, my daddy caught me and put me back in my carrier. And then the plane took off without Karl! Mommy let me look out the window of the airplane. I hope Karl writes to me. I already miss you, Karl.

Goodbye, Karl. I love you.

MARCH 12, 2016

Dear Karl,

I'm all alone and missing you. I'm imprisoned by Chicago snow, and it's so cold.

Love,

Chloe

Dear Chloe,

I miss our walks, and I miss seeing you. I go out into the backyard, and I know you aren't on the other side of the fence. When are you coming back? I love you, Chloe. Come back to me.

Love,

Karl

MARCH 13, 2016

Did you know there is magic in doggy kisses? There are strong healing properties in these kisses that will heal wounds as well as hearts. This magic has been documented many times!

MARCH 29, 2016

I'm wishing for a nice juicy steak with provolone cheese and dark green lettuce.

Wishing for a juicy steak.

MAY 15, 201

Dinner was fabulous: salmon, organic butter lettuce, and organic blueberries. Now that my tummy is happy, I'm thinking about my heart. Chloe, when are you coming back to me?

MAY 17, 2016

I have a job to do. If anyone comes to the door, I'm awake and alert. Otherwise, I'm busy taking a nap. It's exhausting listening for the doorbell, listening for Daddy or Mommy to come home, and greeting people at the door. That's my job, and I do it well. I'm like a butler in a fur coat.

MAY 19, 2016

I wish for everyone a peaceful heart and dreams that are sweet, and dreams that surround you with love. May you always be safe and remember how precious you are and that you are loved more than you know. Goodnight.

MAY 21, 2016

I call Mommy's son, T-Bone, my brother. Yesterday I spent the day at Uncle Marty's house along with Mommy and Daddy. T-Bone and his wife, Angie, were there, too. Mommy and Angie made lunch and . . . shhhh . . . Uncle Marty let me lick his plate! There was some gravy, meatloaf, and mashed potatoes left on his plate. I have never tasted anything so heavenly.

When Mommy figured out what Uncle Marty was doing, she slapped her forehead. When Daddy figured out what was going on, I thought he was going to go apoplectic! But he survived.

And then, when it was dinner time, Uncle Marty put some gravy on my meat. I love being at Uncle Marty's house.

In the evening, everyone watched two good movies and all during the movies Uncle Marty or Angie or T-Bone were petting me and making a fuss over me. What a wonderful day.

JUNE 8, 2016

May everyone have a soft place to land; a place safe and warm, and always welcoming. A place where you are loved completely. I'm in my place—Mommy's arms. There is no other earthly place like it.

In Mommy's loving arms.

JUNE 17, 2016

Mommy, I smell Ponderosa Pine trees. Are we there yet? I can't wait to see my squirrel friends and all the people there and their fur-children! Can Daddy take me for a walk as soon as we get there? I need to go for a walk . . . like now . . .

AUGUST 20, 2016

Today this little guy came to our door. He was alone, and his ears were down and his tail was dragging. Yesterday, Daddy saw a coyote walking down our street going toward the forest. So Daddy

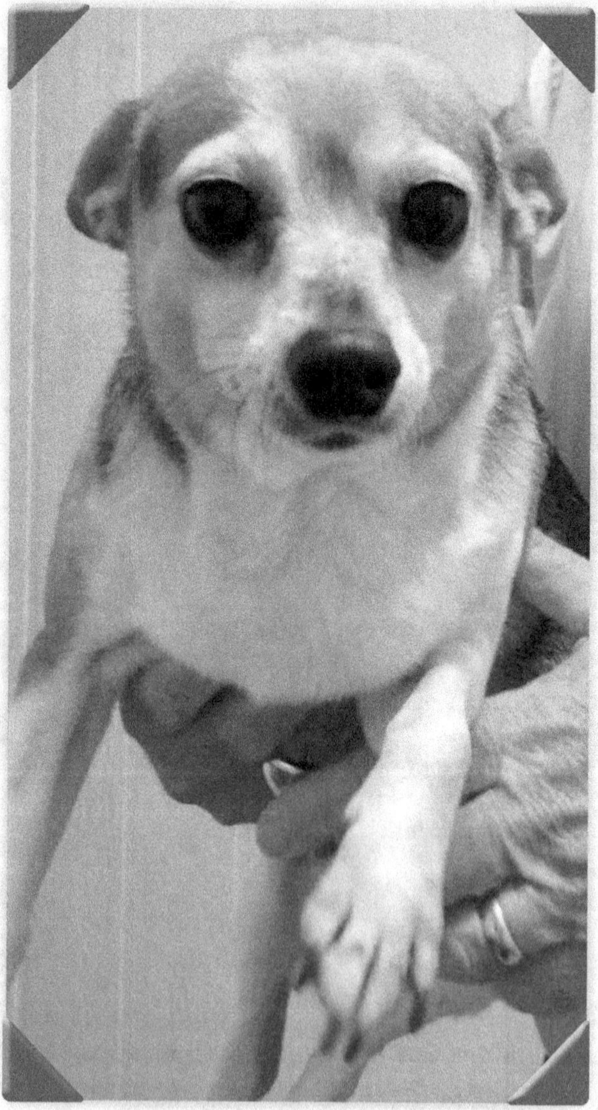

Can we keep Ricky?

scooped him up into his arms. He didn't want this little guy to be a snack for the coyote. Daddy asked Mommy, "Who is this?"

Mommy said, "I think that's Ricky."

I wanted to play with Ricky but Daddy wouldn't let me. I like Ricky! I asked Mommy, "Can we keep him?!"

Mommy said, "No. That's Lucy's brother, and his mommy would miss him."

I was sad. I want a brother or sister!

Ricky's mommy was soon at our door and took Ricky away. Sigh . . . I know what I want for Christmas.

<u>MARCH 13, 2017</u>

Chloe is back! She invited all of us over to her house next door for dinner.

After dinner, my parents were sitting around a table by the pool talking with Chloe's parents. I know that Uncle Rick and Auntie Kim love me as much as they love Chloe. Uncle Rick said, "Why don't I pull the cover off of the pool, and Karl can go swimming?"

My daddy said, "No. Thanks anyway, Rick. Karl's hair is long now, and I don't want him getting a lot of hair in your pool."

What? I can't go swimming? Why not?! I'm a Boykin Spaniel; a bird dog with webbed feet. I went over to the edge of the pool, and Chloe came over to me and said, "Karl, don't go in the pool. You'll die. It's dangerous. I went in one time, and it's not a good idea. I almost drowned!"

I looked at Chloe and said, "Chloe, I'll be fine. Watch and you'll see." I walked around the pool and looked for a good place to jump in, and then I told myself, "Jump!"

Chloe ran to her daddy and screamed, "Karl is going to die!"

My mommy yelled, "Karl jumped in the pool, and the cover is on!"

Uncle Rick leaped from his chair and threw off his shoes as he ran to the side of the pool. Daddy was right beside him. Chloe raced around the edge of the pool and screamed, "Karl! Karl! Karl!"

Fortunately, there was enough water flooding the top of the pool cover, and I was able to swim to the edge of the pool and get out. Whew! I was scared because I was sinking into that plastic.

But here's the good news. Chloe's parents invited me and my parents over for a pool party this Thursday! And Uncle Rick is going to take the pool cover off, and then he is going to have me retrieve some rubber ducks. I'm going to have a lot of fun jumping in and out of the pool. Chloe said she can't watch. Sigh . . . she doesn't know what she's missing by not swimming in her pool.

APRIL 16, 2017

Mommy is trying to take a nap, but she is taking up the whole couch; so I have to get comfortable wherever I can. This is, after all, my couch. Mommy covered up with her nice quilt, and I like lying on top of her quilt. It's soft and comfortable. I could get used to this.

This is the way to take a nap!

MAY 10, 2017

It's baby Leilani! I love her! I'm helping her daddy, T-Bone. Mommy, can we keep Leilani?

I'm helping my brother feed Leilani.

MAY 17, 2017

I thought Daddy was bringing me to Uncle Marty's house, but NO! He brought me to the doctor's office. This doctor made me go to sleep, and when I woke up, there was this cone on my head. Daddy said the doctor took off the itchy fatty tumor that was on my chin. I have to wear this on my head for ten days!

JULY 5, 2017

Oh! I can feel the ice through this cooler. Phoenix is so hot. Mommy said we are going to Flagstaff where we have a house in the forest. I hope I'll see my squirrel friends and my new dog friend, Lucy, on the hill. She is so cute. "Daddy, are we there yet? Could we stop at the rest area? I have to go for a walk!"

SEPTEMBER 23, 2017

Flagstaff is nice this time of the year. Let's see . . . is there anything left on my Flagstaff bucket list today? Breakfast was Alaskan Salmon . . . had a walk . . . saw a squirrel friend and a couple of canine friends . . . came home and Uncle David came by to see me, and then Uncle David talked to my daddy about the gutters on our Flagstaff house . . . Daddy played with me some more . . . went out to the backyard and inspected all the new pine cones that dropped since yesterday . . . watched Mommy fix lunch . . . chewed on my antler . . . went for another walk and checked out all the new smells . . . now Mommy is rocking me on her lap and patting my tummy while she reads . . . it's 1:00 PM and my bucket is empty . . . and I love everyone . . . ZZZZZ!

Yesterday Mommy and Daddy came home with all of these toys! For me?! Mommy said, "Karl, these toys are not for you. They are going to children in a hospital."

But Mommy, you know I love toys. What happened to "He's a spoiled doggy?" Then Mommy took me out of the room so I couldn't even look at the toys. I felt sad. And then they left the house again. Sigh . . . now I'm home alone again, don't know when they're coming home, and can't even look at the toys I can't have.

When Mommy and Daddy came back, Mommy had a plastic bag. Daddy took me out to the backyard and when I came back into the house, Mommy said, "Find your new squeaky toy!"

I looked all over the living room and found not one but *two* new toys that squeak when I play with them! I'm a spoiled doggy.

Stuffed animals for children in a hospital.

What do you mean, "Don't sleep on this pillow?" This is my couch . . . oh, this is Mommy's pillow? Ha! My couch . . . my pillow. Ahh . . . best pillow in the world . . . ZZZZZZZ

Whose pillow?

Mommy's pillow is the best pillow.

JAN 3, 2018

When my daddy goes into his office to meditate, I like to go with him. Tonight, when Mommy and Daddy were eating dinner, Daddy said, "You know what? When I finished meditating this evening, I opened my eyes, and it looked to me like Karl was levitating!"

MARCH 9, 2018

Mommy told Daddy that I need to go on a diet, and she got a doggy cookbook. She put me on a low carb diet. Daddy said, "What's Karl getting for dinner tonight?"

Mommy said, "The same thing we're getting for dinner: baked sweet potato without the skin and brisket with the fat cut off. We can each have our own bowl."

APRIL 9, 2018

Wowzah! Mommy and Daddy went to Costco this afternoon, and they brought back organic strawberries, which were tasty with my doggy meatloaf and cooked carrots. Mommy said Daddy can put some strawberries in his dinner, which is going to be a chocolate smoothie.

JULY 2, 2018

I had a wonderful day with a walk early in the morning when it was cool here and then I played with my toys and had a wonderful dinner of saltless buttered carrots, stew meat, and pinto beans. I sat on Mommy's lap for a while as she read and then I sat on Daddy's lap for a while. Now I'm tired and don't want to get up and walk over to my bed. I'm so comfortable here with my head on the pillow Mommy made. I'll just sleep in this chair.

JULY 28, 2018

Mommy went to bed after lunch today, and I stayed by her side like I usually do. An hour later she was in the bathroom making an awful noise. I asked Mommy what was wrong, and she said she was "tossing cookies."

I ran to get Daddy who was watching TV wearing headphones. I danced with my front paws in front of him and stared at him with my golden eyes. Finally, he looked at me, took off his headphones, and said, "What do you want, Karl?" I ran back to Mommy, and he followed me.

Daddy talked to Mommy as he touched her hair and rubbed her back. Daddy said, "You stay out, Karl."

"No! That's my mommy." Daddy put his leg by the door to try and keep me out, but I squeezed my head between his leg and the door. "Are you going to be okay, Mommy?!"

Finally, Mommy stopped making that awful noise and awhile later Daddy helped Mommy back to bed. He pulled the covers over her shoulders and touched her hair. I was by Mommy's side. Daddy reached over to me, scratched me under my chin, and said, "I'm proud of you, Karl, for coming to get me." He patted my neck. "Watch over your mommy."

I laid down and put my chin on both paws so I could listen with both ears to Mommy breathing. "Okay, Daddy," I said as he left the room.

Are you going to be okay, Mommy?!

OCTOBER 12, 2018

Hurray! Mommy told me Uncle Marty is going to pick me up today, and I'm going to stay at his house for the whole weekend.

I waited by the door for Uncle Marty and pretty soon he was walking up to my front door. I had my seat belt harness on and so when he opened the door I ran out to his car, but then Uncle Marty called me back and said, "We're not going yet. Let's get your treats, Karl."

I came back into the house. "When can we go, Uncle Marty?" "Pretty soon, Karl." Then I heard Uncle Marty tell my mommy and daddy that he had some steaks he could share and would I like some broccoli with my steak for my dinners. And he could scramble an egg and put that on my breakfast kibble. Wowzah!

Finally, Uncle Marty said we could go, and I ran to the door and out to his car. Uncle Marty buckled me in, and Mommy and Daddy stood by the car and waved goodbye.

I'm at Uncle Marty's house now, and while I'm waiting for my dinner, I'm looking out the front door watching for the neighborhood dogs to go by. I bark at them to let them know—I'm back!

During the day Uncle Marty plays with me and takes me for long walks. In the evening we usually watch a movie. It was a little cold today with the door open; so Uncle Marty wrapped himself up in an afghan. I don't need an afghan because I have a fur coat. When I'm beside Uncle Marty, I like propping my chin up on his leg. I couldn't be more comfortable. The movie was pretty interesting, too. Sigh . . . I like being me. I always have such a good time at Uncle Marty's house.

AUGUST 14, 2019

I knew it! I just knew it. When Mommy started whining, "It's so hot! It's sooo hot!" Daddy packed the truck, and we're going to Flagstaff, where I get to see Bunny. She is so cute. She's a little white poodle, and she lives across the street.

SEPTEMBER 28, 2019

Leilani came over and played with me. The game I liked the best was hide-and-go-seek. Leilani hid in the house someplace, and when I found her, she gave me a treat! My treats were pieces of provolone cheese. I love being with Leilani.

Leilani is kind and gentle with me.

NOVEMBER 18, 2019

Yesterday, Mommy and Daddy bought groceries. Mommy got some Angus beef patties for me and something special for all of us to snack on. Tonight, I found out what that snack was— imitation crab meat! When she sat in her chair, I thought she wasn't going to share, but then she gave me some of her snack. Wowzah! I like snacks.

DECEMBER 26, 2019

I got toys for Christmas, and today Leilani played with me. She likes to play "Chase." So I chased her around the house. Then Leilani wanted to go for a walk, but it wasn't a walk. It was a run. I was so tired last night that Mommy said I snored all night.

JANUARY 2, 2020

I learned how to climb ladders before I met Mommy and Daddy. And I was thinking about my girlfriend, Chloe, next-door. I mentioned to Mommy that I would like Daddy to put a ladder up against the cinderblock wall.

Do you know what she said?! "In your dreams, Karl!"

Okay . . . ZZZZZZZZ

Dreaming of Chloe.

APRIL 2, 2020

Mommy and Daddy are back from the store. COVID is going around. They went to Costco and couldn't get in because of the long lines. So no beef patties for me from Costco. Then they went to a small Walmart. When they got home, I looked into some of the bags of food and said, "Mommy, did you get me some beef patties?"

She said, "No Karl. Walmart didn't have any beef patties."

I felt sad. Then she started pulling food out of the bags: lettuce, onions, sweet potatoes. She said I could have some sweet potato for dinner. That would be good . . . but it's not beef. Then she pulled out some deli ham, not for me, some deli roast beef, not for me, cans of kidney beans, and cans of chili, not for me. "Mommy, did you get any salmon or eggs?"

"No Karl," she said. "There were no cans of salmon and no cartons of eggs." THEN she pulled out some packages of meat. Beef! Lots of TOP SIRLOIN!

"Yes, Karl. These steaks are for you. We got a lot of steaks for your dinners."

Holy moly! Hold my squeaky! Wowzah! I did a happy dance.

APRIL 6, 2020

Mommy was up late last night working on a facemask prototype and needed to take a nap this afternoon. My dinner time came up, and Daddy fixed my dinner. He made three hard boiled eggs and put doggy kibble on it. Daddy, you didn't give me a vegetable. You know how much I like veggies. And I haven't had any fruit this week. You know Mommy gives me fruit three times a week.

About an hour later I heard Mommy get up. I ran into the bedroom, did some spins around her and wagged my tail and said, "Mommy, wait until you hear what Daddy gave me for dinner!" I followed Mommy to the kitchen where Daddy was wandering around.

He said, "Sweetheart, what's for dinner?"

Mommy said, "What did you give Karl for dinner?"

Daddy said, "I didn't know what to give him, so I made him hard boiled eggs and put some kibble on top. What are we having for dinner?"

Daddy watched Mommy fix my dinner. Mommy cooked some organic green beans for me and put some sour cream on the side, and then she took out some homemade cornbread, which had a lot of eggs, some organic corn and extra butter added to it. She crumbled up some cornbread and sprinkled it over my green beans and added two slices of a fresh peach. Dinner tasted fabulous.

Daddy had egg salad, cornbread with honey, and peaches with whipped cream.

Mommy never lets me have honey or whipped cream. Why does daddy always get the food I can't have? Sometimes, life is not fair.

APRIL 10, 2020

Mommy supervised my dinner tonight. She made steak for me, just the way I like it—medium rare. And then there were French cut green beans and green lettuce, too. I was kind of traumatized the other night when daddy fixed my dinner without any vegetables, but when I saw the green beans, and Mommy said, "It's steak, Karl," I knew it was going to be a good dinner.

APRIL 17, 2020

I had a special dinner tonight. First, I had beef stew, sour cream, cooked carrots, broccoli, cauliflower, and half of a BANANA! I only get fruit three times a week, and I hardly ever get banana. And then I got a snack of raw veggies: red bell pepper, carrot, and cucumber. So delicious and crunchy.

APRIL 20, 2020

I heard that resting after dinner is good for the digestion. What could be better than resting on my daddy's lap with a full tummy and feeling wanted and loved? Resting on my mommy's lap. I'm a spoiled doggy!

AUGUST 14, 2021

It's true. I'm a mama's boy. When Daddy leaves and Mommy's home with me, I don't even get off the couch to say, "Bye!" I especially won't get off of Mommy's lap. And if Mommy and Daddy leave together, Mommy is Daddy's responsibility.

However, if Mommy goes out by herself, who is going to take care of my mommy? I don't like that at all. The special thing I have is Doggy Radar. This enables me to know how far Mommy is away from me. And when she is five minutes away from being back home, I sit at the door to her garage and listen for the motor of her car. When I sit at the door, Daddy knows, too, that Mommy is almost home.

And best of all, when Daddy hears the garage door go down, he opens the door to her garage and says, "Go see Mommy!" I run out to greet her and walk with her back into the house. All is right with the world.

AUGUST 25, 2021

T-Bone, Angie, and Leilani were here yesterday, and today I'm exhausted. Leilani played with me all the time she was here. I think I lost at least a pound!

SEPTEMBER 4, 2021

I sit by Mommy while she plays the piano. I like to watch her hands and listen to her piano at the same time. I especially like to hear her play "Midnight Sun" and "Afternoon in Paris."

Listening to Mommy's music.

SEPTEMBER 7, 2021

Whenever we travel a long distance, Daddy stops at Burger King and gets me a double burger with lettuce. Hold the salt!

OCTOBER 7, 2021

Mommy is not the same. She has a big bandage on her knee. I follow her everywhere. This is the look I give to her all day. It's a look that will heal her.

My healing look.

NOVEMBER 4, 2021

Mommy had her knee replaced and has a physical therapist at my house three times a week. Unfortunately, there are no pain killers that work on Mommy; so I have to use my special powers. She sits in her La-Z-Boy and puts the foot rest up. Then I jump up and snuggle next to her leg, and she feels better.

Using my special powers on Mommy's knee.

NOVEMBER 17, 2021   🐾 🐾 🐾 🐾 🐾

I should have known this was no ordinary car ride because Mommy wasn't with me. Sure enough, when Daddy parked the car, in big letters was the word "VET." Sigh . . .

When we went inside some nice lady put me on a scale to find out how much I weighed. Hurray! Only thirty pounds! Two years ago, I was thirty-two pounds but it wasn't my fault. I have to eat Mommy's cooking. When I was adopted in 2015, I weighed twenty-five pounds. That didn't last long.

After that Daddy and the nice lady took me to a small room. Then the doctor came in, sat on the floor with me and said, "Hi Karl! It's so good to see you!"

I remembered him and greeted him with a lot of tail wags that were swinging back and forth so hard my whole butt was moving. As he sat on the floor with me, he gave me lots of pets and ear scratches. Then he looked at my eyes and ears, listened to my strong heart, and felt my lymph nodes. He gave me a shot that didn't even hurt.

Then he asked daddy what I eat, and the subject of Mommy's cooking came up. Daddy said I eat beef patties or salmon or eggs, veggies, fruit three times a week, and sometimes sour cream. Then the doctor asked what Daddy eats for dinner. Daddy said, "I eat whatever Karl has left over." Ha! There is nothing left over.

DECEMBER 29, 2021

I have troubles. I got a foxtail between my toes on my front paw, and Daddy took me to the emergency room. I saw a nice doctor who took out that terrible foxtail. After the doctor took out that mean stickery thing, she offered me some cheese she spritzed from a can onto a cracker. Excuse me . . . I only eat the good stuff like provolone that Mommy gives me.

The doctor said, "I guess he doesn't want this."

When I came home, Daddy put a soothing warm cloth on my paw and then Mommy gave me two pills wrapped in provolone cheese. That's more like it!

I had a little problem today. Mommy put my seat belt on and said we were all going for a ride. Mommy knows I like to get out of the house now and then.

Daddy was driving and nothing looked familiar. In a short while, Daddy pulled into a parking spot, left the car running, and Mommy got out of the car. Mommy went around a corner, and when I couldn't see her anymore, Daddy started backing the car out of the parking spot. WHAT? Daddy is leaving Mommy! I started to cry so loud that Daddy stopped the car and said, "What's wrong Karl?"

He pulled back into the parking spot and turned off the engine. He came around to my side of the car and took me for a little walk. We had a man-to-man talk, and he assured me he would never leave my mommy, and we would be back to pick her up. That was okay with me, and I stopped crying.

Daddy buckled me into my seat belt again, and we went to a drive-up window for Daddy's cup of coffee. We were soon back to the place where Mommy got out of the car. It wasn't long before I saw Mommy walking to the car. All is right with the world.

On Saturday evening, February 6, all of my lymph glands were suddenly enlarged. Mommy and Daddy were alarmed and took me to the emergency room at the animal hospital on Sunday morning. The emergency room doctor mentioned lymphoma.

Monday my doctor took an x-ray and my spleen was greatly enlarged and the lymph nodes in my stomach were enlarged, too. My doctor, who loves me, said the humane thing to do was to let me go.

When Mommy and Daddy adopted me, they promised me they would love me forever, and when my time came to pass over the rainbow bridge, they would not let me die alone. Mommy and Daddy kept their promises, and I passed over the rainbow bridge peacefully, without pain, and in their loving arms.

I love you, Mommy and Daddy.

Thank you for adopting me and giving me a good life. Thank you for loving me enough to let me go. And when you say "Goodnight, Karl," I will hear you.

If you are ever feeling down, look into my eyes and know that I love you and all is right with the world.

Charley Here: Breakfast is being served at the Maricopa County Animal Care and Control shelter where there are about five hundred dogs. There are about fifty dogs in my wing, all barking and excited. I'm not barking.

Last December I was found in a park and someone brought me to this shelter. A thousand animals are brought to this shelter every month. I saw a doctor when I first came here, and I got a lot of shots and a microchip put into my neck. After I saw the doctor, I was put into a small kennel, which is about five-feet by five-feet, and I could go outside into a small space. Even though there are a lot of dogs around me, and the caretakers are kind and loving toward me, I feel alone.

Charley Here: Last night a chocolate-colored dog with golden eyes walked into my dream. He said, "Hey kid, of all the dogs in all the towns in all the world, you will be chosen to go to a special forever home. Your hard life is over, and all will be right with the world.

"A man and a woman will come here tomorrow and take you to their home that is filled with love and peace. You will want for nothing and never be yelled at or hit. You'll love the food. The attention and love you will receive will be wonderous and fill your heart with happiness.

A chocolate-colored dog with golden eyes.

"But you should know a few things first. The woman likes to quilt and play the piano. When she quilts, your duty is to keep her company. When she plays the piano, go sit by her. You will enjoy hearing her music and watching her hands. The man likes to read and watch the news.

"Another thing you need to know is that you will be going for car rides wearing a harness attached to a seat belt. You'll get used to it.

"Also, you will have a lot of aunties and uncles—too numerous to mention. They will all love you. One of them, Uncle Marty, will take care of you when the man and woman leave town. Going to his house will be fun, and the food is good there, too.

"Finally, you need to know there is a problem at this house. The woman is crying a lot! The man tries to comfort her by hugging her tight and telling her how much he loves her, and she stops crying, only to start again an hour later. The man says fixing her broken heart is above his pay grade. However, it's not above your pay grade, which is why I have chosen you to go home with this man and woman. Your duty is to fix her broken heart by looking into her eyes with all of the love you have in your heart.

"I'll be watching over you. Here's looking at you, kid."

FEBRUARY 22, 2022

I woke up this morning and remembered my vivid dream and the chocolate-colored dog with the golden eyes. I thought and wondered about this dream all morning. Then, this afternoon a caretaker came to my kennel and put a leash on me. I thought we were going for a walk, but she said, "Okay, Charley, this is your chance to have a nice home. There is a man and a woman who want to meet you."

My caretaker is worried about me because the county can't keep dogs for a long time. And not many people want large dogs like me. I weigh sixty-five pounds. That's small for a Great Dane but no one would call me a small dog. And people don't want eight-year-old dogs like me, either. And then I have a big scar on my forehead and some smaller scars on my head and body, as well as large carbuncles on my elbows from living on cement. I've had a hard life.

I thought back to my dream and what I was told. In my dream, I saw what the woman looked like. The caretaker opened the gate to a grassy compound, and I saw the woman who was in my dream. As soon as she saw me twenty feet away, her face lit up with a smile. She turned to the man and said, "I love his face." I continued to walk toward her and when I was right in front of her, I looked into her eyes—just like the chocolate-colored dog told me to do.

The woman said to the man, "I want this dog." She reached out and touched my face with kindness. She didn't care about the scar on my face, and she didn't care that I was an older dog.

The man looked at the woman and looked at me. He said, "Sweetheart, are you sure? He's a big dog. Much bigger than Karl." The man was not sure if he wanted to take me home. I kept looking at the woman.

Again, she said to the man, "I want this dog."

He said, "But are you sure?" The woman stared at the man and kept petting my face. He said, "Okay, let's take him home. Happy wife, happy life."

The woman was in love with me as soon as she saw my face. I went over to the man, and he touched my face with a gentleness I have never felt before. Now the man was in love with me, too. That took five minutes.

The caretaker who brought me into the compound broke out in a big smile. She said, "He is such a sweet dog. You will love him. We call him 'The Gentle Giant.'" She was bursting with happiness for me. She took me off to get me ready to go to my forever home.

As the man and woman stepped up to the county clerk's window, the man said, "Sweetheart, he's a big dog."

She said, "I don't care. I want him."

A lot of paperwork needed to be signed, and I was adopted under my new mommy's name. The county gave me a special leash and collar with a shiny new tag with a number on it. The clerk changed all of the information that went with my microchip. I had a new name, Charley Winters, and a new home address.

I was waiting outside with two people from the kennel when my new daddy pulled their car up next to me. Mommy was already in the back seat, and I was afraid of the car. It took four people to get me into the back seat. My new mommy stayed in the back seat with me on the ride home.

This is a picture of me on the way to my forever home. I put my head by Mommy's leg. She was petting me and talking to me in a soothing voice all the way home. I was scared.

I'm Charley Winters, and I'm on my way to my forever home.

FEBRUARY 23, 2022

Here's how my day started: Mommy washed my eyes and face with warm water on a washcloth, combed my fur, and put silicone scar cream on the big scar on my forehead.

Then Daddy gave me a cup-and-a-half of good quality kibble for breakfast, and I ate a cup of it. I'm holding out for dinner, which is going to be Angus beef and gravy.

Of all the dogs in the world, Karl chose me.

I love following Mommy around. Karl said I should always be with her. I'm a good boy, too. Daddy said so.

I had a bad dream in the middle of the night, and Daddy got up with me. We had a little talk, and we went outside. I'm okay this morning, especially after Mommy washed my face with warm water on a soft washcloth.

I send everyone much love and wishes for a happy life in which you know you are loved and wanted; a life in which you are with people who will love you forever. I'm excited about having a lot of aunties and uncles who love me even before they have met me. And finally, thank you, Karl, for bringing me to a Mommy and Daddy who will love me forever and be with me until I pass over the rainbow bridge. All is right with the world.

"Goodnight, Karl."

"Goodnight, Charley."

THE END

I'm in my new backyard.

Afterword

Dear Mommy,

I'd not yet seen your face, while I waited those three months,
At a place called Friends for Life, but still recognized at once,
That my mom had come at last, the first moment our eyes met,
And knew from that day forward that, for life, I would be set!

Of course, I wasn't wrong; joy upon joy piled up,
And I lived the days of love and fun wished for by every pup.

I had toy boxes (full!) at our houses in three towns—
And extra special playtimes when Leilani came around.

I made new friends all over—gained aunts, uncles . . . cousins, too;
Some human, others canine—and some rodent (quite a few).

I feasted on fresh veggies, fruits—even filet mignon,
But most special of all, to me, was time spent with my mom.

I listened as your piano made sounds I loved to hear,
And when you went on errands, told Dad when your car was near.

I snuggled up beside you everywhere and time I could,
And pondered whether any other dog had it so good.

But time on Earth is fleeting, as we (of all species) know,
So, far too soon, the time came when I knew I had to go—
Well, physically, that is—of course, in spirit, not apart—
Like I said in that dream—where we can still speak heart to heart.

Still, since I can't be there—well, in that way I was before,
I sought out someone special, and ushered him to your door.

He's not used to the kind of life ("spoiling" some rudely say)
That, thanks to you and Dad, I came to expect every day.

I've told him all about the days of happiness ahead—
Though, it might take some time for him to grasp all that I said—
And told him his new life comes with responsibilities,
Like looking out for mom as chief among his new duties.

I know that he and you will figure out things as you go,
But in the meantime, I've just sent this note to let you know,
I'll be watching all the while, until the day we meet again,
To share days all together, filled with joy and without end.

Your boy forever,
    Karl

—Written by Mil Scott, editor and publisher of *The Rodent
    Reader Quarterly.*

About the Author

Sharon Winters, *a retired teacher* of English and mathematics, is the author of the award-winning memoir *Cutted Chicken in Shanghai,* an exploration of her time living in China, and *Runtie the Desert Rat,* a touching story about the wonders of nature and the spirit of family. Sharon's stories have appeared in *MENSA BULLETIN: The Magazine of American MENSA, The New Mexican,* and *The Rodent Reader Quarterly.* She holds a BS in psychology from Illinois State University and an MA in humanities from the University of Texas. Find her online at www.SharonWinters.com.

The author lives with Charley and her husband in the Phoenix area where she continues to quilt and play the piano. Her next book will be another children's book. This book will be about Charley and his love of quilts. She always remembers to tell Karl good night because real love never dies.